How to Choose a University

University

The Undergraduate Student's Guide for Choosing the Right University

By

Louis Thomas

ISBN: 9781517225292

Contents

1.) Foreword

In September of 2012, I ventured into a new and exciting period of my life when I began my undergraduate law degree at the University of Bristol. I had a fantastic three years. I met some amazing people that will remain life-long friends. I came to understand more about myself, and what I wanted out of life. I learnt how to become more responsible and self-sufficient. I left university with memories that I will cherish forever. Oh, and I left there with a degree too. You know, *that* thing.

Having said all of this, had I known then what I know now about the University of Bristol as a place to study, and the city of Bristol as a place to live, I could have gotten even more out of my degree. With the benefit of hindsight, I can reflect on the time when I was choosing between universities, and recognise the gaping holes that were in my knowledge about both the university I chose *and* its surrounding area. I'm also able to understand how these gaps in my knowledge led to so many aspects of my university experience coming as such a complete shock to me.

For instance, I wasn't aware of just how expensive accommodation in some of the areas of Bristol could be, and I was often bemused why one university in the south west of England seemed to have so many students from London!

Had I been given direction on how to research my list of prospective universities more effectively, and understand what it was that I should *really* have been taking notice of, I could have made a much more well-informed decision, and these aspects of Bristol wouldn't have come as such a shock to me.

Part of the problem with choosing a university for me though, was that I had nobody with first-hand experience of attending university to seek guidance or advice from. I was the first person in my immediate family to ever attend university, and my hometown of Cwmbran in South Wales is hardly a graduate-magnet either. And when you're really clueless about a process, as I was with university, you don't even know what it is that you don't know. There were many aspects to university that had never even crossed my mind until I was actually there.

Looking back, what would have helped me was a guide written by someone fresh out of university providing all of the insights that they'd accumulated over the course of their studies, consolidated into one easy-to-read and accessible document. So, *voilà!* I have taken it upon myself to muster up every bit of knowledge that I've gathered over the last three years, to produce a guide that will hopefully answer all of the questions and concerns that you as a prospective fresher could possibly have when choosing which university to attend.

What this guide *is not,* is a guide concerning all of the technicalities of applying to universities through the UCAS system and all of that jazz. There are already tons of great resources out there that walk you through this process. Applying to university is actually the easy part of the process, anyway. This guide covers the far more difficult aspect of the university application process, which is finding the right universities for you to apply to in the first place. What follows, is a clear step-by-step guide to choosing a university that will be the best match for you as a unique individual.

So here it is. If you've bought this guide, it's because either you or someone you know is hoping to attend university and you're seeking help with choosing which ones to apply to. I hope that it answers every question that you could possibly have that relates to this task. If you're still left with questions after reading this guide, or have any suggestions for a future edition, please get in touch. My e-mail address is: howtochooseauniversity@outlook.com.

It's been a pleasure making this guide, and I hope that you take great pleasure in reading it. If you do choose to attend university, I wish you all the best of luck in this new and exciting stage of your life. Who knows where it will take you. The world is yours.

Louis.

2.) Introduction

In the UK alone, there are over 100 formally recognised universities, offering a combined total of around 50,000 courses to prospective university students. With what is essentially an ocean of possible choices on offer, is it any wonder that many young people are left feeling overwhelmed with the seemingly impossible task of somehow wading through all of these options?

This is where this guide comes into the picture. As someone who has just graduated from university, I have an abundance of fresh advice and insights to offer *you*, the prospective undergraduate university student. In this short and concise guide, I'm going to walk you through the process of narrowing that list of 100+ possible universities down to the *one* university that is likely to be the best possible fit for you as an individual. This will be achieved in five steps:

Step 1: Find universities that offer the right course:
This first step involves drawing up a list of universities that offer the right course for you. For readers who require assistance with identifying the right course, a section of this guide is devoted to this task.

Step 2: Find universities in the right location: Once you've drawn up a list of universities that offer the right course, you'll probably need to narrow that list down by excluding all of the institutions that aren't situated in your ideal type of location. I'll provide you with insights and advice that will help you to determine what kind of location will best suit you during your time at university.

Step 3: Research your shortlist of universities: When you have a list of universities offering the right course in the right location, it's time to research your remaining shortlist of universities. You'll learn where to find the right resources for this task and how to use them. I'll also share my insights with you on the statistics that *actually* matter.

Step 4: Weigh everything up: Step 4 involves weighing up all of the information that you've accumulated thus far to help you make a final decision about which university to choose. I'll provide you with the knowledge that ensures you give weight to the *right* factors during this process. I'll also provide you with a method to use for the task of weighing everything up.

Step 5: Choose a university: The fifth and final step concerns reaching a decision about which university to apply to. I'll provide you with the definitive way to choose a university. I'll also provide you with some final thoughts and pointers regarding the application process, before you click that "submit" button on your UCAS application.

And then you'll be finished! By the time that you finish reading step 5, you will have chosen a university to attend. Rest assured that it will be the best possible decision that you could make, as it will be providing the right course, in the right location, and everything that you've researched about it will align with all of your preferences and desires relating to how you envision your ideal university experience.

So without further ado, let's head straight into the main content of this guide. Before proceeding to step 1, however, there are some very important preliminary points that we must first address.

3.) The Importance of Choosing the Right University

So why does this book need to be written? Why bother reading a book about choosing a university when you can quite easily browse through the UCAS website for half an hour, select five universities that seem okay, and send your application off on that same day? Well, here is my rationale:

It's a financial decision. A BIG financial decision

This is a very important factor that many people fail to appreciate, because when we go to university we're often very young and underestimate the financial impact of university attendance. An 18 year-old won't necessarily give a second thought to the idea of having to eventually pay back the fees years down the line. But if you speak to the 30 year-old who is still taking a hefty wage packet hit paying a 'graduate tax' for a university degree that has absolutely no relevance to their current job, you will understand the true impact of the costs involved.

Choosing to attend university is one of the most important and expensive decisions that you will ever make in life. Just as you wouldn't enter lightly into buying a car or a house, you shouldn't enter lightly into a university course either. Remember, these fees will affect you for *years*. You'll still be paying them off long after you graduate, and they might one day affect whether you're able to buy that house or car that you want. Choosing the right university will help ensure that the money you plough into your university education turns out to be a worthy investment.

It will affect the next 3-5 years of your life

This point cannot be underestimated either. The decision to attend university will affect where you're going to live and what you'll do with the majority of your time for the next 3-5 years of your life, depending on the length of your degree. So it's important that you spend several years of your life doing something you enjoy in a place that you like. Otherwise, the years could be long, gruelling and miserable. And you're never going to get those years back either.

Degrees aren't what they used to be

This third point is not intended to scare people away from pursuing a degree. They can be amazing tools towards high quality, high-paying jobs and the career of your dreams. However, I stand by the statement that degrees are not what they used to be.

Rightly or wrongly, the result of the 1997-2010 Labour Government's education policy of widening access to university is that around 40% of young people now obtain degrees. Of course, if nearly half of all people now acquire a qualification that only 1 in 10 people used to achieve, then employers aren't going to be as impressed, since it is less 'special' and rare and you're less likely to stand out amongst a pile of CVs. Therefore, it's imperative that you make your choice of university and degree course count.

4.) Is University Right for You?

Even though this is a guide that focuses on *how* to choose a university, which essentially presupposes that you've already decided that university is the right choice for you, I must emphasise as strongly as I can that there *are* other options out there. For a very large number of people in this country, university may not be the right choice. I want you to critically reflect on *why* you are choosing to attend university, so that you can determine whether it's actually for the right reasons or not.

So it's worth asking whether university is right for you because the answer could be a resounding *no*! Many people are now wising up to the fact that university isn't a safe bet anymore. Many graduates are finding themselves in jobs that they could have obtained without spending the past 3 years at university, and without the £27,000 worth of debt that they would have amassed because of that.

One must remember that sixth forms, colleges and universities all have their own agendas to push. You're lining their pockets, so of course they're going to want you to think that you *need* a university education in order to succeed in life. It's not in their interests to inform you that there are other, possibly better, options out there for you, because they depend on you to sustain their existence.

So how do you know if university is right for you? The most important consideration is your reason for wanting to go to university in the first place. You have to ask yourself what your underlying motivation is for wanting to go there.

As a general rule, there are only two valid reasons for attending university. But before I touch on these, I want to cover the *wrong* reasons to choose to attend university.

The WRONG reasons to choose university

The wrong reasons to choose to attend university are:

You have no other direction in life

I've already briefly touched upon this. University is too expensive to be used as a way to fill the time when you don't know what to do with yourself. With £9000 tuition fees per year, along with the cost of food and accommodation, even spending a gap year in a foreign country works out to be a far cheaper option. Of course, I'm not saying that you need to know exactly what you want to do with your life at the age of 18. I'm just saying that you can't afford to *not* think about it either.

The chances of you just picking a random course to study at university, then working out what you *actually* want to do with your life, and having that course coincidentally align with your newly-discovered aspirations are slim-to-none. The more likely scenario is that by the time you realise what it is that you want to do, your degree will turn out to be almost entirely irrelevant to these new aspirations. You'll then be spending a significant portion of your life paying off this irrelevant qualification.

Do you know what I have found to be the best source of inspiration? Working at a boring 9-5 job. Even better if you *hate* it. Just a few weeks of putting yourself through the hardships of the 'real world' will give you a supercharged resurgence for discovering what it is that you want to do with your life, simply as a way of escaping the hellish routine.

Doing something that you hate or find really boring also gives you plenty of opportunity to daydream about the things that you would prefer to be spending your time doing, and to realise what really brings you joy and satisfaction in life.

For the sole purpose of making more money

It's hard to argue against the fact that on average, graduates will earn more than their non-graduate counterparts. However, there are two points to take into consideration about this.

Firstly, this is a statistic that is delivered in terms of averages. It does not apply to all individuals, and so just because you choose to go to university, doesn't guarantee that you'll earn more money in your lifetime than if you didn't.

Secondly, there are other ways that money can be made without ever having to attend university. In fact, many of the richest people in history became rich through entrepreneurship and making their own money. This often doesn't even require a university degree, so don't fool yourself into thinking that university is the only path to financial success in life.

The student lifestyle

By all means, enjoy the student lifestyle as part of the overall university experience. However, don't choose to attend university exclusively for the sake of being able to laze around for three years.

Honestly, I know that a socially acceptable lifestyle of dossing around until the afternoon and watching Jeremy Kyle every day sounds quite pleasant. And for the first few months, it really is. But believe it or not, at some point you will actually grow tired of a diet that consists of beans on toast every day, and where the only alcohol that you can afford to buy is a nasty supermarket's own brand that tastes like paint thinner. As I said, this is part of the novelty that is the student experience, and it is to be enjoyed. But if this kind of lifestyle is your primary motivation for wanting to attend university, then I advise that you re-evaluate these motivations.

To gain independence

Gaining independence can definitely be a big perk of university, and there are very few people who would contend that they didn't become more independent as a result of their university experience. The point I'm making here though, is that if the main reason that you want to go to university is simply to get out of the house and away from your annoying parents, then there are less expensive ways to do so.

You could choose to work abroad for a few months, or even take the plunge and get a job so that you can afford your own place. That way, you can get that time away from home that you so desperately crave, whilst also earning an income. For example, I spent the summer of 2014 working at a summer camp in the USA. Along with all of the independence that came with that, I also managed to walk away from the experience with a positive sum of money in my pockets. The same cannot be said for going to university.

The social life

Some people say that they want to attend university because of its social aspects. They want to go to epic parties and things of that nature. This really makes me laugh because there are far, *far* better ways to achieve a buzzing social life than by spending £27,000 to spend a large portion of three years sitting in silent libraries revising for exams.

Yes, university will provide you with an abundance of free time, and with many interesting people from all over the world to become acquainted with. But honestly, if socialising is that important to you, then you could work at a bar in Magaluf and party as much as you like, and you wouldn't be piling yourself into tons of debt in the process either.

No matter how organised or intelligent you are, success in your university exams and coursework *will* require a portion of studiousness. University cannot be 24/7 socialising and partying without major sacrifices being made in the grades department. So just bear that in mind.

Pressure from other people

You shouldn't be going to university for anyone other than yourself. I know that for some parents, hearing from their child that they don't want to go to university might be contrary to their own vision of what was in store for you. But that's *their* problem to deal with, not yours.

At the end of the day, your happiness trumps your parents' expectations. I think that most parents come to accept any decision that you make over time, anyway. One way to guarantee that you'll have a horrible time at university though, is to go there for the primary purpose of appeasing other people in your life.

The problem is, those other people won't be doing the work for you. Your parents won't be spending all of those hours in the library. Your friends won't be sitting those exams in the summer. They won't be paying off your university debt either. You should be doing those things because *you* want to, not because other people want you to.

As I've already mentioned, there are plenty of ways to become a financial success that don't involve attending university. So if your worry is that you can't make your parents or the rest of society proud without obtaining a degree, then rest assured that you definitely *can*. But also remember that even if you wanted to do something which wouldn't make them proud, then that's also completely fine. Life is about what *you* want to do.

These lessons don't just apply at the macro level of life directions and career choices either. They also apply at the micro level of matters such as your choice of university. Don't feel that you have to apply to Oxford or Cambridge just because your older brother did, or because it's always been a life-long dream of your parents to have a child go there. If you have the desire to attend what is considered to be a 'lesser' university because it suits you and your preferences, then don't let the opinions of anyone else get in the way of that.

The RIGHT reasons to choose university

Since I've provided a list of the *wrong* reasons to choose university, it only makes sense to now provide a list of what I consider to be the *right* reasons to choose university. There are only two of them. These are:

A university degree is required for your Ideal career

There are some careers in which a university degree is a prerequisite. Obvious examples that come to mind are doctors and vets. This is probably the best reason to choose to go to university. The degree course is related to your career aspirations, and so any debts that you incur now can be treated as an investment for the future.

Since the degree is related to what you want to do in later life, it should also provide you with the necessary impetus to really push yourself and try to succeed at your course, as it will be directly applicable to the career that you aspire towards.

For the love of the subject

The second reason that you should ever attend university, is for the love of the subject that you wish to study. This might also be extended to the love of academia or learning in general.

In the past, university wasn't seen quite so strongly as the qualification churner that it is today. Instead, it was perceived as the go-to place to explore a subject that you were passionate about, in an environment that provided you with like-minded individuals and knowledgeable tutors to support you in doing so. It's still lovely to promote this idealised notion of the university education experience.

However, despite this reason being one of only two that I have regarded as acceptable for choosing to attend university, even this one is debatable. You see, unlike past generations, we now have access to the internet. We are capable of accessing almost the entirety of the world's collective knowledge from the comfort of our own homes.

Of course, there's no comparison between solitarily reading information from a computer screen, and sitting in a room full of other people who possess the same passion for a subject as you do. But it's worth remembering that you could probably access most of the information that the degree is providing for free on the internet.

So really, the unique selling point of the university experience (other than providing you with a qualification), is the facilitation of a unique opportunity for like-minded people to come together and share ideas. You have to ask yourself whether that's worth the extortionate fees that universities charge for their degree courses.

If you really are passionate about a subject though, or academia in general, you should probably go to university regardless of the fees. You'll be spending several years of your life doing something that you love, and that's not the kind of thing that you'll ever come to regret.

In this chapter, we've covered both the right and wrong reasons to attend university. If your personal motivations for attending university fell into my category of "wrong" reasons, then I strongly suggest that you reflect on them. Try to make your motivations applicable to one of the "right" reasons that I provided. If you are unable to do this, then I would *strongly* recommend that you ask yourself once again whether university is right for you.

If your motivations and desires for attending university *did* correlate with what I called the "right" reasons, then I invite you to now read on to the next chapter, where we will finally get to the details about how to choose a university to attend.

5.) How to Choose a University

It's time to get to the heart of this book, which addresses the issue of choosing a university to attend.

As stated in the introduction of this book, this task will be achieved in five steps. These steps comprise of: 1) finding universities that offer the right course; 2) finding universities that are in the right location; 3) researching them; 4) weighing all of the considerations up; and 5) making the final decision about which university you'll list as the firm choice in your university application.

These steps are all in chronological order, so the first step that we'll cover is finding universities that offer the right course.

Step 1: Find universities that offer the right course

Our first step involves finding universities that offer the right course. This requires you to have already identified what the "right" course for you actually is. I would hazard a guess that the vast majority of people reading this book are yet to have done this, and so a large portion of this step will actually be geared towards helping people identify what the "right" course for them is.

Once you've worked out that part of the equation, the rest of this step will be fairly straightforward. All that you'll have to do then is draw up a list of all of the universities that offer that particular course.

How to find the right course

For those of you who seek assistance with identifying the right course to study, the answer to this dilemma lies in a very straightforward, but not easy, question.

What is your passion?

This is perhaps the most difficult question to answer in the whole of this book. It often takes a surprisingly long time to think of what it is that you're really passionate about. Fortunately for us though, we've already addressed this question. Kind of. In the '*Is University right for you?*' section, I said that you should only ever attend university as a stepping stone for a dream career, or for the love of a particular subject.

Whatever came to your mind when you read through that section, is the passion that you can identify here to determine which course to study at university. If your ideal career is to become a civil engineer, then you know that the course that you should study is civil engineering. If you spend all of your spare time reading fictional stories, and have a blog where you post critical reviews of everything that you read, then an English literature degree might be the perfect choice for you to facilitate the passion that you have for reading.

You might have more than one passion. You might have dozens of passions. And there might be several jobs that you would consider to be dream careers. In which case, don't perceive this as a stressful situation where you have to somehow try and choose one 'right' option. Instead, engage with this task whilst coming from a place of abundance.

You're fortunate enough to have several things that you're passionate about, and so no matter which decision you make it will be the 'right' one, because any of the options that you choose will be something that you enjoy. Framing the issue in this manner helps to take all of the unnecessary stress and worry out of the equation.

Conversely, you might feel like you don't really have any passions. That's fine. A very large number of people at university will be studying something that they're not particularly passionate about. In which case, you can simply tone the question down and ask yourself what interests you, and proceed to identify courses that facilitate those interests.

Now that you've identified your passions, you can use them to steer you towards identifying possible courses to study at university. Once you think that you've identified a possible course, you can use the questions below to further guide you in reaching a decision.

Will you get the grades for the course?

It goes without saying that you have to be capable of achieving the necessary grades for your desired course. If you want to study maths at the University of Cambridge, with typical offers demanding A*A*A at A-level, then you're going to be in trouble if during your AS-levels you achieved ABC. Even amongst the universities that set lower grade requirements for their courses, offers consisting of Bs and Cs will be difficult to meet if your grades are currently in the D range.

 Another factor that has to be taken into account is that some subjects, such as medicine and law, will carry high grade requirements at *every* university, regardless of prestige, due to their popularity. So even if you're an A-grade student, which is highly respectable and deserves a pat on the back, there might be some courses that will be off-limits to you if you aren't capable of achieving the very, very top grades at the A* level.

The final thing that you should also take into consideration is this; if the typical offers corresponding to that course would require non-stop work on your behalf to achieve the minimum grades necessary to qualify, is it a wise idea to aspire towards that course? Think about it, if you have to work *really* hard towards a subject during your A-levels, to the extent that it affects other areas of your life, just to minimally qualify for that course, then it's only going to get *even harder* for you at university.

Let's use an example. Say that you want to be the next Albert Einstein. You love physics, but it just doesn't come naturally to you. You love science, but you're not necessarily scientifically minded. If you have to work day and night in order to achieve the 'A' grade at A-level that your university's physics course demands, to the detriment of your social life, then university is only going to be more difficult. It's going to disrupt the equilibrium of your life even further, and perhaps might not be worth it in the long run.

The key is to find something that you're passionate about *and* naturally suited towards.

Have you got the right A-levels for the course?

Now don't shoot the messenger, but it's worth pointing out that some universities are very prejudiced towards certain A-levels that schools teach. Therefore, even though you might have the grades that the universities are asking for, it's worth checking just to see if your prospective university has a 'blacklist' of subjects that they refuse to consider. If a university does have such a blacklist, you'll normally be able to find it on their website.

Also, whilst some degree subjects such as law are open to people with virtually any variety of A-levels, others will require a specific set of A-levels. For instance, you're not going to be accepted onto a medicine degree if you didn't take any science subjects, even if you achieved A*A*A* in History, English Literature and French. So do check that the A-levels that you have, even if you have fantastic grade scores in them, actually qualify you for your preferred degree course.

Are you satisfied with the course outline?

Most universities have course outlines that you can view beforehand. I highly recommend that you take a look through them. Even though it's very easy to skip this when you're so busy with your A-levels, it's really important to just set aside that bit of time to understand what it is that you're signing yourself up for.

University courses aren't standardised in the same way that A-levels and GCSEs are. The courses that universities offer can vary widely in content, even if they go by the exact same title. Without taking the time to check beforehand, you might not find out until you're actually at university that the one module that was really important to you, and that you really wanted to study, isn't on the syllabus.

University courses will differ in other ways as well. For instance, the opportunity to study abroad for a year is very important for some people, and so if you're one of those people then you will want to ensure that any prospective university course offers this, and that the nature of the year abroad is something that actually appeals to you too. Some courses might only offer one semester abroad, while you want to spend a whole year abroad. A prospective course might only offer the opportunity to study in Spain, when you want to travel to South America to exercise the language skills that you developed during your Spanish degree.

Another reason that it's important to check the outline of the course is because different courses will be assessed in different ways. Some universities might rely heavily on examinations as their preferred method of assessment, whilst other institutions may choose to provide more opportunities to be assessed by means of coursework. If you absolutely hate exams and relish the opportunity to be assessed by means of coursework, then it would be wise to check that the course that you're considering affords you that opportunity, and vice versa.

Will the course make you more employable?

You have to be very careful with the use of this term, because whilst some subjects certainly boast fantastic employment rates (such as medicine, with a whopping 99% employment rate), you can't generalise amongst most degree subjects. For example, you can't *necessarily* say that a maths student is more employable than a media studies student. The maths student might have terrible social skills, a bad attitude and a nasty personality. Even with a 1st class degree from Cambridge, they would still be virtually unemployable.

Setting that aside, the most important consideration is how the degree relates to what *you* want to do after university. For instance, whilst the maths graduate has the odds in their favour for a banking internship application in the city of London, it will be the media studies graduate who has the advantage in applying for a media planner vacancy.

This is why it's important to have a long-term vision about why you want to go to university, and what specialist knowledge and skills you want to leave it with, having paid a fortune to acquire those skills. To try and avoid this situation, you could try to pick a generally respected degree with 'transferrable skills', but then this takes us back to square one, which is that you shouldn't subscribe to a degree course that you're not particularly interested in, just for the sake of employability. You could arguably get away with this by studying a generally respected degree with transferable skills that you are genuinely interested in though.

Draw up a list of universities that offer the course

Once you've worked out which course you wish to study, you need to draw up a list of universities that offer that course. This can be quickly and easily achieved by accessing the UCAS search tool at http://search.ucas.com. Just enter the title of the course that you wish to study, and you'll be provided with a full list of all of the universities that provide it.

By the end of this step, you should now have a list of all of the universities that provide you with the course that you wish to study. Don't worry if you have a relatively large list at this point, as there is still a *lot* of scope for narrowing it down in the upcoming steps.

Step 2: Find universities in the right location

The next step in choosing a university involves finding universities that are situated in the right kind of location, both in the pure sense of the word and also referring to the surrounding characteristics and facilities of a university. Ensuring that your university is in the right location is important because you'll be spending more time there than anywhere else for the duration of your degree. You don't want to spend three years in an environment that you're not fond of, as that can have a dampening effect on your overall university experience.

Locations for universities can vary wildly. Some can be situated at the hearts of the biggest and most populous cities in the whole of the UK, such as the University of Manchester and the London School of Economics. Others are situated far away from the cities and into the countryside and seaside areas, such as Aberystwyth University in Wales.

There are many different elements to a university's location, and they should all be taken into consideration. In no particular order, I've drawn up a list of questions to ask yourself that concern these various factors relating to the location of a university.

Is the cost of living suitable for you?

A very important consideration relating to a university's

location is the cost of living in the surrounding area. Everyone has their own budgets, and some people's are much larger than others. Not everyone can afford to live in central London, where people don't bat an eyelid at paying £600 a month towards rent.

London is notoriously more expensive than the rest of the UK. Whilst it is true that London students are awarded larger student loans than elsewhere, this rarely covers the enormous disparities in the costs of living. The question that I would invite you to ask yourself (and this applies no matter where you're thinking of heading for university, not just those who are considering applying to a university in London), is could you enjoy a decent standard of living there?

Remember, you're there for three years. Do you really want to have to spend the whole time worrying and watching where every single penny goes, or would you rather just be able to live happily in a place where you don't have to worry about money so much? Sure, you might have to make the sacrifice of living in a place that isn't quite so swanky, but I know which one I would choose.

Consider the distance from home

The distance from home that people are comfortable with when they go to university varies widely. Some people want to go as far away from home as physically possible. Others decide that staying home would actually be the right choice for them, and so they choose to commute to university every day, instead of moving into student accommodation.

You then have the plethora of options that lie somewhere between those two polar opposite choices. Each of them have their own pros and their cons, and so you have to think about which one would best suit *you*. Here are some things to bear in mind when you do so:

What if you get sick or personal tragedy strikes?

Trust me, being sick when you're away from home is always *horrible*, whether you're one mile away or 1000 miles away. However, the further away from home that you are when this does happen, the lonelier you can feel. After all, as kids we always relied on our parents to make us feel better whenever we were sick.

You have to consider whether you would be the type of person to easily cope if you were to become ill or if something tragic were to happen back at home. If you were the type of person that would just *have* to go home on such an occasion, then it's probably not worth applying to universities where this would be difficult to do so.

Homesickness

A lot of people will already have an idea about whether they have a tendency to suffer from homesickness or not. By the age of 18, many students will have spent at least a small amount of time away from home on school trips and what not.

However, there will be some people who have never spent any time away from home, and so won't know whether they're susceptible to it or not. It's important for these people to bear this in mind when choosing a university, because they're going to be stuffed if they realise that they suffer from homesickness when their home is in Portsmouth and they're going to university in Newcastle.

Campus or non-campus?

You'll want to consider whether you want to attend a university with a campus or not. The obvious perk of a campus university are all of the benefits that come along with having all of your facilities being centralised in one place. It's particularly handy during your first year. Your classes are very close to your accommodation, and you get the opportunity to be in close proximity to virtually all of the other students in your year. *"How could there possibly be any downsides to a campus university?"*, you might ask.

Well, for a start, consider when you're in your second or third year of university. You're no longer in the halls of residence that are conveniently situated within the confines of the campus. Instead, you'll have to find private accommodation elsewhere outside of the campus. For some universities where the 'hub' of the university campus is isolated from the nearby town or city, this can create quite some distance and inconvenience.

The other issue is that some people feel a little bit suffocated by the campus format. After all, sometimes it's nice to just take a break from feeling all 'studenty'. Being part of the 'normal' areas of a town or city, surrounded by all of the different mixes of people from all stages of life, helps in dealing with this.

So weigh up the pros and cons of each of the two options to decide which you prefer, and then you know which prospective universities to rule out based on this preference.

What is the nightlife like?

Making sure that the universities and their surrounding areas can provide you with the kind of nightlife that you desire is another important step. After all, none of the universities expect you to be spending the entirety of your degree being chained to a desk in the library. The universities themselves actively encourage students to let their hair down during their free time, so it's important to consider how you would choose to spend yours. Ensure that whichever university that you're thinking of applying to can then facilitate that.

If you're the type of person to go clubbing several times a week, and enjoy having a wide array of venues that play difference genres of music to choose from, then it's probably not the best idea for you to go to somewhere with only a very limited number of clubs. You're going to get bored *very* quickly. You'd be better off going to the larger cities such as Bristol, Birmingham or Manchester for this purpose.

Perhaps you don't enjoy clubbing, and would prefer a nice old-fashioned pub instead. Again, you want to check around to see if that kind of pub culture *actually* exists in the area, otherwise you could end up being bitterly disappointed to find that your only options on a Friday night are nightclubs that sell nasty drinks and charge extortionate entrance fees.

Conversely, you might not be a drinker at all. In that case, the number of pubs and clubs on offer will be an irrelevant consideration for you. Instead, you will want to consider what other facilities a university might have which would be of particular interest to you.

Recreational Facilities

Along with the kind of nightlife that a university's location provides, it's also worth thinking about the kinds of recreational facilities that are on offer at any prospective university.

A fairly common example would be something such as a university gym, but there are more unique and obscure facilities that may be on offer to you at certain universities. For instance, the University of Exeter has its own cinema, and the University of Durham has its own theatre.

Wherever your interests lie, there is probably a university that can accommodate those interests, either through a facility hosted by the university itself or via the surrounding area.

Surroundings - urban or rural?

Everyone has their preferences. Some people love the city. Others love the countryside. It would probably be wise to ensure that your choice of university reflects these preferences. After all, you will be spending the next three years living at your chosen university, so it's highly beneficial if you can actually enjoy and appreciate its surroundings.

Of course, you aren't just stuck with choosing between the giant, overcrowded city and the desolate countryside.

There's a whole spectrum in between for you to choose from, depending on whether you lean more towards urban or rural environments. There are even some universities that offer a very good mixture of both. Places such as Bath and Exeter come with all of the perks of living in a city, whilst also providing you with the kinds of beautiful scenery that the countryside provides.

Every area of the UK has its own character, and it's up to you to either travel to these places, or research online as much as you can to ensure that you gain an accurate 'feel' of them. Once you come to realise the precise kinds of locations that you're fond of, the task of determining which universities are in the right location for you becomes all the more easier.

Remove all universities that are NOT in the right type of location

We must now bring together all of the progress that we've made thus far back to the task of choosing a university. When you completed step 1, you compiled a list of universities that offered the right course. In order to complete step 2, you must now narrow down that list even further by removing all of the universities that are *not* in the right type of location. As a result of doing this, you'll now be left with a list of universities that offer the right course *and* are in the right kind of location for you.

At this point, you'll be left with a fairly small list of universities, with the size of it being dependant on how picky you are. Some people will only be left with a list of two or three universities, whilst others will have 10 or more still remaining. The next step is to start researching all of the remaining universities on that shortlist.

Step 3: Research your shortlist of universities

The next step is to start researching the universities that remain on your list after steps 1 & 2. The information that you gather from your research will assist you when the time comes to weigh everything up to decide which university to choose.

Just performing the task of researching alone will be a very effective and natural way of narrowing down your list even further. As you learn more about each of the universities, you can strike off the ones that don't accord with your preferences. It is entirely possible that by the end of this step, you could even narrow that list down to your single chosen university.

This step begins with an introduction to the resources that will be of use to you when carrying out your research.

Resources

There are literally hundreds, if not thousands, of resources at your disposal. In this section, I'll be listing the very best of these resources for you to use when researching a university. These are:

Push

Push is one of the best resources that I have found for researching universities, and was extremely helpful for me when I was choosing a university. The self-proclaimed "ruthlessly independent university guide" is an all-around excellent online resource that is very easy to navigate and use, so I'm not going to waste any time explaining how to use it. However, I do want to spend a little bit of time highlighting what are, in my opinion, two of the best and most useful features of this website.

First of all, they have detailed profiles of *every* single university, and they are *thorough*. Not only do they include a host of statistics related to the university, but they also provide really neat descriptions of both the universities themselves and their surrounding areas. To give you an idea of just how detailed these university profiles are, they even provide an index of average beer prices.

Secondly, they have a really great tool called the 'University Chooser'. It asks you a bunch of questions, and then using the answers that you provide, it determines which university would be best suited to you. Not only is it fun, but it's also surprisingly accurate and useful. I highly recommend trying it out for yourself. The best part about this tool though, is the interactive map that enables you to 'keep' or 'dump' certain parts of the UK. This is a super effective way of identifying and excluding all of the universities that don't fall within a suitable radius from your home.

The Student Room

The Student Room provides you with a forum for both current and prospective students from virtually every university in the UK to discuss all kinds of topics. This forum gives you the opportunity to read the answers to questions that other people have posted, as well as allowing you to ask your own questions and await for current students to help you out.

For instance, do you have a question about X hall of residence at one of the universities that you're thinking of applying to? Then the chances are that there's either an existing thread dedicated to your question, or you can create a thread yourself and there will almost certainly be other members on the forum who will have attended that university that can help you out and answer that question for you.

I'm not just recommending this resource solely for the purposes of researching universities either. It's also just generally a fun and entertaining forum to be a part of.

The UCAS Website

The big daddy itself. *UCAS (Universities and Colleges Admissions Service)*, is essentially the middle-man between you and the universities. Since UCAS is the only way that you can actually apply to universities, it pays to get well acquainted with its website.

However, don't think that this website should only be used for when you wish to send off your application. The *UCAS* website is an incredibly useful resource that has shedloads of great information to offer you. It contains a definitive list of all of the universities in the UK, and a list of every single course that they offer.

Their search tool allows you to search for any subject, and you will be provided with a list of all of the universities that offer a relevant course, along with useful details such as the length of the course and the precise qualification that it's providing. It really is an invaluable resource. Make sure to utilise it.

League Tables

As I said in the introduction of this book, every university is different. This will inevitably mean that some universities will be better than others. There are a number of league tables, also known as 'University Guides', that attempt to rank all of the universities against each other, and present them in a neatly laid-out table for your viewing pleasure. Examples include the *Times University Guide*, the *Guardian University Guide* and the *Complete University Guide.*

Later on in this book, I discuss some of the pitfalls of league tables. Nevertheless, they're valuable for providing you with a very general idea of how your prospective universities rank against each other and the rest of the universities in the UK.

Facebook

Who knew that the website that we all spend far too much

time wastefully browsing through could actually be put to productive use? With a little bit of ingenuity, Facebook can actually be put to *amazing* use towards the task of acquiring information about prospective universities.

For instance, every university will have its own Facebook page. It will often feature lots of pictures, far more than the prospectus alone will ever be able to provide, and this can be a decent substitute for visiting a university if you're unable to do so. Also, the people that have 'liked' the page will typically be current or ex-students that you could easily send a message to if you have any general questions to ask about the university.

If you have more specific questions to ask, Facebook can be utilised for this purpose too. For example, if you were to have a question relating to a specific hall of residence at that university, then there's a very strong likelihood of it having its own dedicated Facebook page that you can use to your advantage. Want to ask people about Hiatt Baker Hall at the University of Bristol? Simply type '*Hiatt Baker*' into the search bar, and you'll immediately be presented with the hall's official Facebook page. All you would have to do then is post a question on the page and wait for someone to respond to it.

Alternatively, if you would rather be a little bit more discrete, you could simply send a message to any of the people that have 'liked' that page, as it is likely that they will know the answer to whatever question that you have to ask about that hall of residence. The exact same principle applies to societies, subject departments and practically anything else that you could think of.

We've just covered some of the resources that are at your disposal when researching a university. Together, these resources will provide you with more information than you'll ever possibly need to make an informed decision about which university to choose.

The sheer amount of information that these resources will provide you with can be overwhelming, and it might be hard to determine which information is actually useful or not. This is why I've devoted the next section towards telling you precisely which information is worth paying attention towards, and which isn't.

The statistics that *really* matter

In this section, I'll be providing you with the inside scoop on the statistics that *really* matter. As you go through these statistics, be sure to apply the ones that I argue *do* matter, to your own list of universities that are currently remaining. Don't be afraid to strike off universities from your list if they repeatedly score poorly on the statistics that relate to your preferences.

Student satisfaction rates

Do they matter? *Yes.*

This is the one factor that I didn't value enough when I was choosing a university. Looking back, it should have been one of my most prioritised considerations. Why do I say that? I say it because this is the one statistic that will shed light on the kind of *experience* you are likely to have at university. Remember, you'll be paying £9,000 a year, for three years, to fund this 'experience', so shouldn't it *at least* be a pleasurable one?

It's true that the student satisfaction rates of a university are never going to affect your employability. It's also true that some league table ranking systems don't even consider this statistic to be worthy of being included. It would be quite easy to altogether dismiss student satisfaction rates as being a bit of a 'soft' and irrelevant statistic to take into consideration.

That is until you discover that all of the rooms at your university's residential halls are damp and mouldy, and you find out that you're only going to be receiving around three contact hours a week. Oh, and even though you want to spend the day away from your mouldy room, you can't, because there are no spare seats available in the library for you to do your work. These kinds of issues really can take a toll on you, and can negatively affect your whole university experience.

That's why it's so important to check student satisfaction rates. It's all well and good attending a reputable university, but if your experience there is going to be dreadful, then you have to ask yourself whether it's worth it. These years have the potential to be the best years of your life, so make sure that your choice of university doesn't ruin that.

A very important point to make though, is that these two factors are not mutually exclusive either. There's nothing stopping a university from offering a reputable degree course whilst also offering its students a great time during their degrees. Just because a university is reputable, doesn't give it the right to do a poor job of providing a valuable experience to its students. So don't think that you have to choose between one and the other.

If student satisfaction scores are low, something is going wrong. It is worth investigating why students are dissatisfied to see if this would affect you or not. If the reason is because the student union doesn't arrange enough social events, and you don't really like going out anyway, then it doesn't matter. But if it's because students aren't happy with the quality of teaching, and you're desperately hoping for a first-class honours degree, then you might have to consider a different university.

A lot can be said for student satisfaction rates. Whilst having a prospective university scoring highly in league table categories such as research is handy, at the end of the day you'll be experiencing the university as a student, so it's important that your student experience is an enjoyable one.

League Table positions

Does it matter? *Yes, but not as much as you might think.*

Whilst league tables are undoubtedly important for providing a rough idea of the overall quality of an institution, there are three reasons why they're not as important as you'd initially think:

1.) There's discrepancies between tables.

At times, there are noticeable differences in the rankings of universities between tables. For instance, in 2013, The University of Buckingham was ranked 16th in *The Guardian's* league table, whilst ranking 55th in the *Complete University Guide's* league table that same year.

If league tables can have discrepancies as significant as 39 places, then their accuracy comes into question. The University of Buckingham is just one example, and I'm sure that there are other universities with similar discrepancies in terms of their positioning amongst the various league tables.

What perpetuates the issue even further, is that positions can fluctuate each year as well. You could even face the bizarre scenario where in one year a university has improved its ranking according to one league table, while having its ranking reduced in a different table.

2.) The differences between similarly ranked universities are arbitrary.

If you're torn between one university that is ranked 29th in the UK, and another which is ranked as 31st, there's not a big enough difference between the two institutions to actually be of any use or significance.

Employers certainly won't choose one candidate over the other solely on the basis that the one candidate went to the university ranked 19th in the UK, whilst the other went to a university that was ranked 17th. And the better you are as an all-round individual in terms of skills and positive personality traits, the less important the ranking of your university becomes anyway.

3.) They're only highly accurate when dealing with the very best and worst universities.

League tables are only highly accurate when it comes to assessing the very best and worst universities in the country, yet this will be precisely what we and your future employers *already* know. You don't need to check the league tables to know that Oxford and Cambridge are considered to be two of the most prestigious universities in the country, for instance.

Once you get past the top tier of universities, it becomes more or less a grey area. Again, this is where discrepancies between tables can vary wildly too. If you're not going to a top-ranking university, or one of the universities that are considered to be among the worst in the country, then the ranking won't be entirely accurate.

Male-to-Female Ratio

Does it matter? *No.*

I know what you're thinking of. *Trust me*. But in all honesty, you won't notice any difference at all when you walk down the street or around campus. Besides, it all depends on the course that you're studying and how you're choosing to spend your free time.

For instance, you might be going to a university with a student population that comprises of 60% females and 40% males. But if you're studying a subject such as physics, which traditionally has a far greater proportion of males studying it than females, then you're going to be spending all of your 'university time' in an environment where the ratio is more likely to be around 80% male and 20% female. And these course-specific ratios are pretty consistent amongst most universities. In other words, you're probably never going to find a physics course with more female students than male students.

Ultimately, the male-to-female ratio of a university is meaningless because it generally won't ever be noticeable. Instead, differences are more pronounced amongst the courses themselves.

Research Rankings

Do they matter? *No.*

Don't be fooled into thinking that just because a university scores highly in terms of the research that it conducts, that this would necessarily benefit you in any direct or meaningful way. Remember, just because somebody is a good researcher, doesn't mean that they will be good at conveying that information to you.

Of course, there will be some perks to being part of an institution that has renowned research facilities. For example, it means that the tutors will have a world-class and cutting-edge knowledge of their subject. However, whether that knowledge will be of any use to you is questionable. For instance, if you're studying biology, your tutor could be the world authority on morphology, but if you're studying a unit in palaeontology then it probably won't be of any use to you at all.

Having said that, there are also some potential disadvantages to being part of a leading research facility. For example, your tutor could be so invested in his or her own research that they could inadvertently neglect the duties that they owe to you as your tutor.

I must quickly emphasise though that this is not my experience at all. When I was at university, every single one of my tutors were able to balance their research and tutoring duties very well. Not once did I ever feel that any of their researching duties were being disruptive or detrimental towards my education.

Another consideration to make with regards to research facilities, is that your standard undergraduate degree will probably not require any specialist research facilities. Often, the most sophisticated research facilities at a university will be reserved for its PhD and Masters students. The broad, unspecialised nature of undergraduate degrees will never require such expertise, so you wouldn't truly benefit from these kinds of facilities until you were studying towards a postgraduate degree anyway.

On the whole then, research facilities do not matter very much because they would be largely unnecessary during a standard undergraduate degree, and there would be no guarantee that your tutor would be researching anything that's related to what you're actually studying. Unless you're considering pursuing a postgraduate research degree, it is not necessary to pay too much attention to this figure.

6-month employment rates

Do they matter? *No.*

The problem with this figure, is that there's so much context missing from it that it's effectively useless. After all, it tells us how many people are in employment, but what kind of employment? Surely it would be valuable knowing whether this employment was relevant to the degree or not, and whether the employment was in graduate-level jobs as well.

For instance, I would consider a 70% employment rate that consists of high-paying graduate jobs to be far superior to a 100% employment rate comprised of low-paying, entry-level jobs that do not require a degree-level qualification.

The statistic is also skewed by the thousands of students who deliberately choose to *not* head straight into employment following university. For example, many people choose to spend a few months travelling abroad after they graduate. This would obviously skew any employment rates that were being recorded because these people are *choosing* to be temporarily unemployed, rather than desperately struggling to find jobs. Therefore, the employment rates aren't shedding any light on their *actual* employability in this context.

Another factor that can skew the employment rates are those who opt for some kind of further education after their undergraduate degree, either in the form of a postgraduate degree or a professional qualification of some kind, such as the LPC (Legal Practice Course). This is another example of intentionally choosing to remain outside of employment and runs contrary to the picture of thousands of graduates struggling to find jobs, which the statistic may suggest when taken at face value.

This is one of the statistics that, initially, appears to be one of the most important, but in fact is one of the biggest farces. Whilst it has already been explained how there are many factors that skew the statistics in the first place, you should also take note of the fact that they are generalisations that in no way apply to you as an individual.

Just because 80% of students at a particular university find a job within six months, doesn't necessarily mean that you will. Whilst they are favourable odds, you might be one of the individuals that fall into that remaining 20% of people who won't. It all comes down to individual circumstances and what *you* can offer to a prospective employer, which is why these statistics are meaningless in the first place. Going to Oxbridge doesn't guarantee that you'll be able to walk into a great job with your eyes closed, and even attending the worst ranked university in the country doesn't prevent you from landing the most fantastic job that you could ever imagine.

Student-staff ratio

Does it matter? *No.*

Similar to what I said about the male-to-female ratios, you should pay more attention to the student-staff ratio of *your specific course* than your university as a whole, because the ratios will vary wildly between different subjects.

Even setting that issue aside, I'm going to stick my neck on the line and suggest that the student-staff ratio of a university is *not* worth paying much attention towards. This is because the vast majority of your time at university will be spent either in lectures or independently studying - two occasions where the student-staff ratio is irrelevant.

Admittedly, the ratio does become more important in the context of tutorials and seminars, where smaller student-staff ratios allow for greater levels of interaction between each student and the tutor. But in my opinion, even if you were to find yourself in a fairly large group for a seminar, your ability to interact with the tutor wouldn't really be compromised.

At the end of the day, if you're the type of person who likes to speak out and interact with the tutor, then I assure you that you would still have the opportunity to do so even in a large seminar group of 20-30 people. And for those who are a bit more shy, and don't like to speak in front of everybody, larger groups can actually be beneficial in this instance because you're less likely to be 'picked on' by a tutor to answer a question.

Therefore, aside from any truly outstanding ratios, such as the 1-on-1 tutor meetings that some universities are known to provide, student-staff ratios shouldn't be a major consideration of yours. They're a kind of bonus. An icing on the cake. You wouldn't go to a restaurant that served terrible food just because they offered a free dessert. Think of a good student-staff ratio in a similar light.

Percentage of students that achieve a 2.1 or above

Does it matter? *YES.*

This statistic is particularly important, because everybody goes to university with the intention of achieving a 2.1 standard degree or above (even though approximately 1 in 3 students will fail to do so). One way to try and maximise your chances of achieving that gold-standard degree classification, is by subscribing to a university course that has a proven track record for delivering high percentages of 2.1s or above.

If a university does achieve a high percentage of 2.1s, then of course something is being done right, or at least something is being done that works to your favour. Either the teaching is excellent, or the course is easy. The opposite applies too. If there are low percentages of 2.1s being achieved, then either the teaching is poor, or the course is incredibly difficult. In which case, it sucks to be you for the next 3 years.

Of all of the statistics, this one is potentially the most important one to take notice of. Having said that, remember the point I made about generalisability in relation to employment rates. Hypothetically speaking, even with a 99% success rate of 2.1s or above, you could still find yourself in the remaining 1% that don't achieve that. And even with a 1% success rate of 2.1s or above, you could be a part of the 1% of students that actually manage to achieve that grade (although I very much doubt that a department would continue running a course with a 1% success rate for very long!). This statistic is merely an indicator of what you should expect to achieve if you were to put the effort into your degree.

Narrow differences between universities, such as a 79% rate at X compared to an 81% rate at Y, should not be of any major concern to you. In these kinds of instances, whether you achieve a 2.1 or above will be totally down to you. All that you're really looking for is any major warning signs. I'd say that a good yardstick is around the 70% mark, although ideally you'd be looking for 2.1 rates at around the 75-80% mark in order to feel truly secure.

UCAS points and grade entry Tariffs

Do they matter? *No.*

As far as you're concerned, you should only ever pay attention to UCAS points when it comes to determining whether you have enough of them to meet the standard conditional offer that a university typically hands out to people. Otherwise, the "average number of UCAS points per student" statistic that is featured in some league tables is useless. There are two reasons why:

1.) UCAS points aren't strictly academic.

There are several means of acquiring UCAS points other than through the traditional academic avenues. For example, from Grade 6 upwards, you can acquire UCAS points simply through playing a musical instrument! These have no bearing on your academic ability to deal with a completely separate and unrelated course. Just because you can play the violin well, doesn't mean that you can ace a chemistry degree.

2.) There's no relationship between the number of UCAS points required and the difficulty of the course.

Rather than the UCAS point requirement of a course being related to its difficulty, it's more a case of supply and demand and largely reflects the popularity of the course. For example, I know someone whose offer to study chemistry consisted of Bs and Cs at A-level, whilst my offer to study law was AAA. Nobody would contend that a law degree is any great deal more difficult than a chemistry degree. Rather, the law degree was just in such high demand that the university could ask for higher grades as a way of filtering out the large number of applicants.

This principle isn't just limited to particular courses either, it can apply to universities as a whole, too. A university can be incredibly popular without necessarily offering quality courses. In which case, the university can demand higher grades, even though the degree courses offered by that university aren't as demanding as the UCAS point requirements might suggest they are.

Drop-out rates

Do they matter? *No.*

Drop-out rates are another statistic that I wouldn't advise you to pay much attention to. The reasons that people choose to drop out of university are often very personal, and can have little to do with the university itself. For example, a student might be severely missing their family or friends. In fact, I would contend that the vast majority of people are actually willing to put up with a sub-par university experience, simply to avoid the inconvenience that comes with dropping out of university.

Most universities have drop-out rates of around 1-13%, so there isn't a great deal of difference between them. All that you need to look out for are any major causes for concern, such as a university with drop-out rates exceeding 18% or so, because if almost one in five students are feeling the need to drop out of that university, then there's almost certainly something going wrong somewhere down the line with that institution.

Aside from that, there's little to deduce from the statistics, apart from sympathising with the fact that personal crises affect us all at some point in our lives, and this can include our time at university.

Student population size

Does it matter? No.

This statistic only matters if you have a preference for either a bigger or smaller student population. Some people like the fact that in the universities with larger populations, there's a practically endless number of new faces and people to meet. Conversely, other people may prefer universities with smaller student populations, so that they can actually feel like part of a close-knit community. Either way though, as I've already emphasised, this is all down to personal preference, and won't affect your education at all.

Once you have researched your remaining universities...

At this point, having now researched your remaining list of universities, some of you may already be in the situation where you are able to choose precisely which university it is that you wish to attend. After compiling a list of universities that provided the right course, in the right location, your research led you to conclude that *X* University is just perfect for you. That's awesome. You don't even need to read the rest of this book anymore. You're done.

However, for most people, it will not have been that straightforward. Life rarely is. The more likely scenario would be that post-research, you're now left with about two or three universities that you're still clueless about as to how you're going to choose between them. They could be so similar, or so completely different, that you just don't know how you're going to make a decision. This is where step 4 comes in. It's time to learn how to weigh everything up.

Step 4: Weigh everything up

You now have all of the information that you could need to make an informed decision about which university to choose. However, you might find yourself having a bit of a hard time trying to narrow down a list of remaining universities that are all very pleasant, and all of which generally provide the kind of university experience that you're looking for.

You're going to have to find a way to choose between them. The only way that you're going to be able to do this, is by critically reflecting on what it is that you truly desire from a university. That's why the next step to take is to weigh everything up. You're going to have to decide which factors are most important to you, so that you can give the most weight to them in your decision. This involves a consideration of all of the different factors that have come into the equation thus far, along with some new ones which we'll go through shortly.

This step will start with a list of the *wrong* factors to take into consideration when weighing everything up. There will be another section dedicated towards prompting you to think of your own personal considerations to weigh up. After that, I'll be providing some wider considerations for you to take into account. Finally, I'll provide you with a practical and easily applicable method for weighing everything up.

The wrong factors

There are many legitimate factors that you could take into account when it comes to weighing everything up. However, be wary. There are some factors out there that might initially seem fairly reasonable and important, but in fact should be accorded little to no weight at all. Let's explore some of these factors, to show you what I mean.

Your friends are going there

This can seem like a big deal before university. After all, what better way to ensure that you're going to have friends at university than by simply bringing your old ones along? There's absolutely nothing wrong with going to the same university that your friends might also be coincidentally attending. However, if the main reason that you're considering going to a university is because your friends are going there, then that's a *big* no-no.

For a start, you have to remember the reasons that you're going to university in the first place. You're going there to build knowledge and skills towards something that will hopefully aid you in some kind of career after you finish your degree. Just because a particular university might be the right place for your friend, it doesn't necessarily mean that it's the right place for you. It might be fantastic for a music degree for instance, but if it has a terrible science department and you want to study physics, then you shouldn't compromise your (very costly) education just to be with them.

Also, one of the most rewarding aspects of university is

getting to mix with all of the different kinds of new and interesting people who you would never otherwise encounter. If you're hanging around with your friends from back home all of the time whilst at university, then you're potentially obstructing yourself from doing this. You get to spend all of the summer, winter and Easter holidays with your friends back at home, so why not try your hardest to get to know some new people during your time away at university?

Another one of the best parts about university is being granted the opportunity to have a fresh and exciting new start! For the first time since you were about five years old, you have the potential to be in an environment which is full of completely new people who have no preconceived notions of who you are. You can carve out a completely new identity for yourself that better represents who you are than that dreadful nickname from year 9 that has lived with you throughout the entirety of your secondary school education. If you have your friends with you at university, then they'll be bringing with them that box that they've already placed you in, and this will undoubtedly affect new peoples' perceptions of you as a result.

By all means, make sure to maintain relationships with your friends from back at home. If they happen to choose the same university as you, that's fine. I'm not suggesting that you should actively try to *avoid* attending the same universities as people that you know. But make sure to attend the university that is the best place for *you*, not anyone else. And if you do go to university with your friends, ensure that you don't cling to them; make sure you get to meet as many different kinds of people as possible, as this is one of the best opportunities in life to do so.

Your partner is going there

For those who are in a relationship before heading off to university...I hate to break it you, but the chances are that you probably won't make it. Then again, I'm sure that you already know that, anyway. Anecdotally, I can tell you that out of all of the dozens of relationships that I've known where at least one of the partners were heading to university (including my own relationship), nearly all of them failed. Of course, that's not to say that you definitely won't go the distance, but the odds are stacked against you.

Bearing that in mind, you have to best prepare yourself for the possibility that you might, and probably will, break up. It would be very unwise for you to compromise missing out on your ideal choice of university, just so that you could be with your partner. If the worst-case scenario were to happen, you will break up with him or her in your first year of the course. In which case, you'd then be stuck in your less-than-ideal university for the remaining three or four years of your degree.

Besides, similar to the point that I made about choosing a university because your friends are going there; university is a chance to meet new people, and spending all of your time with your significant other could affect that. You don't want to be seen as 'that' couple - the pair that are never seen without each other, and who don't make any effort to socialise with anyone else other than each other.

This isn't a book on relationships, and I don't profess to be an expert on them *at all.* But I do firmly believe that this age is a time for all of us to explore all of the opportunities that present themselves to us to the fullest. If a fantastic opportunity presents itself to you, you should not consider passing on that just for the sake of a relationship which, at this age in particular, isn't likely to last. If you're really meant for each other for all of eternity, you can survive being in a long-distance relationship for a few years whilst you grow and develop as individuals by attending the right university for each of you.

Family tradition

Just because your mum or dad went to a particular university, doesn't mean that *you* should have to go to that same one too. You are your own person, and just because a place suited your parents doesn't mean that it will necessarily suit you.

The chances are that your parents will be looking back on their time at university with rose-tinted spectacles, and there may have been problems with the university that the nostalgia has caused your parents to forget. That's not to mention that institutions can change over the years, for better or for worse. Just because a university was good in your parent's time, doesn't mean that it is now.

So, make sure that you don't choose a university *just* because your mum or dad went there. Recommendations and anecdotes from other people can be useful, especially from your parents. But make sure to choose a university based on an objective analysis of your personal preferences. Do *not* choose a university out of feeling some kind of illogical allegiance to an institution, simply because your parents attended the same place a quarter of a century ago.

Sports clubs and societies

For the sporty types who want to be members of the most revered university sports teams in the country, or those who wish to join a niche society that isn't readily available at other institutions, I would suggest that you do *not* choose a university based on this consideration *alone*. Of course, if you're at a professional or semi-professional level for something then it will rightfully play a very important part in your decision, and it can be a useful way for anyone to distinguish between two similar institutions. But generally speaking, the sports clubs and societies on offer at a university should not be the main influencer in any decision that you make.

After all, you're not spending your £9k a year to join the rugby club or the sauerkraut-making society. Those fees go towards your tuition. Unless you actually have ambitions of becoming a professional athlete, or setting up your own business selling home-made sauerkraut, the quality and content of the degree at that university should take precedence over any extra-curricular activities that it might provide.

There's nobody saying that you can't still enjoy those side-lines as hobbies, and there's also absolutely nothing preventing you from joining any local clubs in the area that aren't tied to the university. You might find that you can join a local sports team, or there might be a group or forum of people on the internet that meet in your local area that share the same passion as you. If there isn't already a society for your passion at a particular university, you could even consider setting one up once you get there too!

The right factors

Now that we've covered the wrong factors to consider, it's time to start thinking about the right ones. We've already touched on some of these, particularly during the research stage, where we covered some of the general statistics that are worth giving weight towards such as student satisfaction rates and the percentage of students that achieve a 2.1 or above. Adding on to these, it's now time to devote a section towards constructing a more personal and tailor-made set of considerations to draw upon.

Personal considerations

In weighing up your considerations, it's worth crafting your own kind of criteria that is uniquely applicable to your personal circumstances. For obvious reasons, I'm not really in the position to do this for you. My advice though, is to have a quiet sit-down, and just try to note as many ideas that you can think of that relate to your everyday life.

You want to think about broad areas of life, such as your health and hobbies. You might have special dietary requirements related to Irritable Bowel Syndrome, and so having health shops nearby that cater to these requirements would be handy. Perhaps you're a huge fan of playing lacrosse, and in an ideal world there would be lacrosse facilities for you to enjoy at your university. Think about as many of these different kinds of factors as you can. Here's a fictional list that provides you with even more ideas.

1.) I have a rare heart disorder. Is there a hospital near the halls in case something were to happen?

2.) I'm an ale enthusiast. Any good pubs that serve quality ale in the local area?

3.) Do the courses at this university come with a sandwich industrial year, so that I'm able to gain valuable work experience?

4.) If one of my favourite musicians were to tour around the UK, is there a venue near the university that they would be likely to attend?

5.) Does the university offer any private accommodation of its own to let to second and third year students, so that I can avoid any greedy and exploitative private landlords?

We've just gone through some personal considerations that you might wish to take into account. It might also be a good idea to reflect on some wider considerations that might aid you in your decision-making.

Wider considerations

You could start examining some wider considerations to help you in weighing everything up. By "wider considerations", I mean looking far and wide into your post-university life to gain valuable insights. For example, is the surrounding area of the university somewhere that you would be happy to live and work in one day? This is an important question to ask. Universities often have strong ties with local businesses, and so you'd be more likely to get your foot in the door amongst those businesses that are in the area where you obtained your degree.

As with the other sections of this step, you can tailor these wider considerations specifically to accord to your life. Think about the kind of life that you aspire towards in your post-university life, and think outside the box to try and find ways that your choice of university could assist you in achieving that idyllic lifestyle.

Now that we've covered all of the different kinds of factors that have to be taken into consideration when weighing everything up, it's time to actually look at the process itself. How do you weigh all of these factors up? Below, I provide my own method for performing this exact task.

How to weigh everything up?

From the outset, it's worth saying that you don't *have* to follow a method this systematic in order to be capable of weighing everything up when choosing a university. Many people are perfectly capable of doing all of this in their head, and without doing so in such a methodical fashion. Intuition alone could perform all of this for you.

That being said, this is a book that's specifically addressing the question of how to choose a university, so it's only right that I provide a formulaic method for those people who do wish to approach the task in such a way. After all, some people are just very methodical in their thought processing, and gravitate towards structured ways to perform tasks. The reason that I would endorse this method specifically, is because it enables you to "score" universities, which is very useful as a comparative tool for assessing your remaining selection of universities. Let's go.

Firstly, you'll want to choose a nice round number as the total score that you'll be rating the universities out of. For the sake of simplicity, let's say 100. Then, using the advice provided in this book, combined with the input of your personal preferences, draw up a list of however many factors that you wish to take into account when weighing everything up. Note that you can also include some of the personal factors that you just listed in the previous section of this step.

Based on the weight that you wish to accord to these different factors, you'll then want to assign to each of them a proportion of that original round number. You can even subdivide these factors into further categories if you wish. Let's pretend that I choose five main factors to give weight towards, with some further subdivisions amongst them too. Since my total score is out of 100, I will be according proportions to these factors that should all add up to 100 when totalled.

The five factors that I have chosen, and the corresponding weight that I will accord to them, are the course (30), the location (30), the proportion of students that achieve a 2.1 or above (10), the position in league tables (10), student satisfaction rates (10), and the hip-hop scene there (10).

Together, these all add up to 100. I've accorded the most points to the course and the location of the university, because they're the highest on my set of priorities. I'll further subdivide some categories amongst these two important factors to enable greater specificity when scoring. I'll demonstrate what this looks like with an example:

1.) Right course? (30)   - Interesting content (10)
                          - Employability (10)
                          - Difficulty of achieving requisite

grades (10)

2.) Right Location? (30)   - Affordable (10)
                            - Close to home (10)
                            - Nightlife (10)

3.) Proportion of students that achieve 2.1s or above. (10)

4.) Position in League Tables. (10)

5.) Student satisfaction rates. (10)

6.) (Personal consideration) Somewhere with a great hip-hop

music scene. (10)

After you have drawn up this set of weighted factors, you will then want to score the universities accordingly. This can be achieved by utilising the information that you gathered during your research in step 3. Once you have assigned a score to each of these factors, you can then tally up all of the scores, and it will leave you with a total score for that particular university.

For example, the fictional University of Scottsville might have scored like this:

1.) Right Course? (22/30)   - Interesting Content (8/10)
                             - Employability (7/10)
                             - Difficulty to achieve Requisite

Grades (7/10)

2.) Right Location? (23/30)   - Affordable (10/10)
                               - Close to Home (5/10)
                               - Nightlife (8/10)

3.) Proportion of Students that achieve 2.1 or above. (8/10)

4.) Position in League Tables. (6/10)

5.) Student Satisfaction Rates. (8/10)

6.) (Personal Consideration) somewhere with a great Hip-

Hop Music Scene. (4/10)

Total Score: (22+23+8+6+8+4) = 71/100.

As you can see, the University of Scottsville has achieved a score of 71 out of 100 through the application of this criteria. You would then apply the same criteria to all of the remaining universities on your list. By the end of this process, you'll be left with a score for each of them. These scores will reflect an effective 'weighing up' of all of the factors in relation to each of those universities, and you can use these scores as a guide to determine which institution to choose.

Once you have performed this task, you will have effectively completed the fourth step of weighing everything up when choosing a university. You will now have a clear idea in your mind about which university is best suited to you. The fifth and final step that beholds you is the act of choosing a university. It's time to make a final decision and send off your university application. Exciting stuff!

.

Step 5: Choose a university

First off, I just want to say congratulations for reaching this step! You've drawn up a list of universities that provide the right course for you, and you've whittled that list of universities down to the ones in viable locations. You've then researched all of those universities. Armed with that information, you've narrowed that list of universities down even further. Stage 4 enabled you to critically weigh up your options. All that's left for you to do now, is to choose a university. By the end of this step, provided that you have followed the guidance carefully, you *will* have come to a final decision about which university you'd like to attend.

Those of you who followed step 4 may already have your answer about which university to choose. But for those who are still not sure, the next section will provide you with a cut-throat approach to choosing a university. This is a method that is guaranteed to enable you to narrow your list down to one remaining university.

The cut-throat approach to choosing a university

1.) Draw up a List of "deal breakers"

First of all, you need to draw up a list of "deal breakers" that can be construed from the kind of factors that were considered in step 4. This list can be as long or as short as you like, but I would recommend trying to think of as many different "deal breakers" as possible. Don't go feeling guilty about demanding something that seems almost embarrassingly specific or difficult to achieve either. This just makes it even easier to narrow down your list.

2.) Rank the deal breakers

Once you have created this list of deal breakers, you will then want to rank them in such a way so that the most important ones are listed first, and the less-so-important deal breakers are situated towards the end of the list.

3.) Apply them to each university

Once you have a clearly ordered list of deal breakers, you will then simply apply these to each of the remaining universities on your shortlist. If a university "passes" by virtue of fulfilling the criterion of a particular deal breaker, then it goes "through to the next round", to the next deal breaker that is ordered on your list.

As this process continues, there's two ways that a university can emerge as the "winner" from applying this method.

Firstly, one remaining university may emerge as the winner by virtue of the rest of the universities failing to meet the demands of your list of deal breakers. You might have drawn up a list of seven deal breakers, and by the sixth one, you had just one university left standing. There were no other universities that were capable of jumping through the hurdles that you had set. In which case, this university would automatically qualify as the "winner".

Alternatively, there might be more than one university that succeeds in meeting the demands of the entirety of your current set of deal breakers. In this instance, you will then reapply that list of deal breakers, whilst setting a stricter element to their criteria.

So, if one of your previous deal breakers were that the university had to be within a 4-hour drive, you might make this stricter by requiring it to be within a 3-hour drive. By doing this, you can tailor the requirements to your exact needs. Eventually, this will leave you with just one university remaining, and this is the one that you should choose to attend. It will be the best possible choice for you.

For demonstration purposes, I'll go through the situation that I was in three years ago. I had three remaining universities to choose between. They were the University of Bristol, University of Birmingham and University of Exeter. Some of the kinds of deal breakers that I listed when I was trying to choose a university were:

1.) Had to offer a course in law.
2.) It had to be outside of Wales. (I fancied a change)
3.) It had to be within a 3-hour drive.

As some of you may have noticed, these three particular 'deal breakers' were useless for narrowing this list down any further, because they were all offering a course in law, all outside of Wales, and were all within a 3-hour drive. So I had to think of something else.

I looked at the location requirement of having to be within a 3-hour radius. As far as I was concerned, the closer the better. After all, if I was feeling unwell, or had to rush home for whatever reason, this would be easier to do if I was an hour away, than it would be if I was three hours away. So I decided to alter that requirement, and narrow down the criterion of the distance to within a 90-minute drive.

This alone ruled out both the University of Birmingham and the University of Exeter, leaving me with only one university left, the university that I eventually attended; the University of Bristol. So for me, just making that one deal breaker a little stricter enabled me to finally narrow down that list from three prospective universities to one.

I highly recommend this kind of rigorous process of elimination as a method for finally deciding upon a university. Not only does it enable you to reflect on the factors that really matter the most to you, but it ensures that the one remaining university that you'll have on your list will be tailor-made to your exact needs and suit you better than any other university could.

Now that you know which university it is that you wish to attend, it's time to start thinking about sending off your application. This begins with a quick word about the UCAS application process, with reference to your possible choice of 'firm' and 'insurance' universities.

UCAS: Firm and insurance choices

Even though I said that this wasn't a book about how to *apply* to university, I just want to touch on the 'firm' and 'insurance' dimensions of the UCAS process.

As part of the UCAS application process, you will have to assign one university as your 'firm' choice, which will be your first choice of university. You'll then have to assign another university as your 'insurance'. This will serve as a back-up, in case you're unable to secure a place at your firm. This is so that you if you fail to achieve the necessary grades specified in your conditional offer, or if your firm choice chooses to cancel the course for whatever reason, you'll still have a plan B to fall back on. Let's cover each of these in a little more detail.

Your firm choice

It goes without saying that your firm choice should be the university that you have the greatest desire to attend, as this will be the institution that you'll be automatically enlisted upon on results day if you manage to fulfil the conditions of your offer.

You should ensure that you are actually capable of achieving the grades that your firm choice asks of you. There are few things more gut-wrenching than to be rejected by your dream university on results day, as a result of failing to achieve the requisite grades.

It is incredibly important that you are totally happy with your choice of firm, because it can be an absolute nightmare to try and correct this situation if you were to have a change of heart. If you did have a change of heart, and had already received a conditional offer from your insurance university, then you would have to seek agreement from your firm choice for them to "reject" you, so that you could be passed on to your insurance choice.

Just take your time, and make sure that you choose the right firm in the first place to avoid a lot of hassle.

Your insurance choice

Your choice of insurance university is as important as your firm choice. If you fail to get into your firm choice of university, at least you have a back-up plan in the form of your insurance university. But if you fail to gain entrance into your insurance choice of university, after you have already failed to get into your firm, then there is no back-up. There is no plan B. No safety net. You're then forced to enter into the very uncertain world of clearing, in which you could potentially be left empty-handed, with no suitable university course to subscribe to.

Therefore, even more so than with your firm choice of university, it is absolutely essential to ensure that you can achieve the grades that are being asked of you by your choice of insurance university.

The most important thing to bear in mind about your choice of insurance university, is that you should actually be happy and willing to attend there if you were to fail to secure a place at your firm choice. After all, this is the university that you would be enlisted upon if that were to happen. It's nonsensical to select a university as an insurance choice if you wouldn't have any genuine intention to attend there. All that you'll be doing is depriving other people of the opportunity to attend that university by hoarding offers.

If there truly is no other university that you would be happy to attend other than your firm choice, then simply don't select an insurance choice. You're well within your rights to do so. Then, in the event that you do fail to secure a place at your firm of choice of university, you can choose to either apply again next year, or choose to venture into an entirely different route in life other than university. To reiterate a message that's been conveyed throughout the entirety of this book; there's no point in paying a fortune in tuition fees to attend a university that you're not 100% happy and excited to attend.

That's all that I'm going to say about your firm and insurance choice of universities. In the final section, of this final step of the book, I'm going to impart some final nuggets of advice.

Final nuggets of advice

I'd like to impart some final nuggets of advice to you that relate to sending off your application.

Reminder: It's YOUR decision

To echo the sentiment that has already been expressed a thousand times in this book, the decision concerning which university you'll apply to is *your* decision, and *yours alone*.

Whilst there may be wise insights coming from many directions, the decision should ultimately be your own. Even if your parents are the ones who will be funding your university education, this is an adult decision that is to be made by *you*, since it is *your* life that it's affecting.

Take your time...but not too long

Don't panic! The worst thing that you can do is make a rash decision with little forethought and end up regretting it. You only have the opportunity to make one UCAS application per year, so make it count. You have ample time to ensure that you carry out enough research before you send it off.

Having said that, it's also important to remember that the window of time in which to apply is finite. Whilst there are official deadlines to adhere to, it's worth pointing out that many universities hand out offers well before these official deadlines. In fact, offers can be dispensed as early in the year as October.

This is why it's critical to make sure that whilst you're taking your time, you're not wasting it either. It would be a terrible shame if your dream course ran out of vacancies whilst you were busy doing a whole lot of nothing. So try to ensure that you send your application off well in advance of the stated deadlines. Just make sure you do so in a calm fashion. Don't rush!

Be happy with your decision

No matter what your decision is, just be happy with it. Of course, upon pressing that "submit" button, a little bit of anxiety is inevitable. But it's really important to decipher between these perfectly fine feelings of anxiety, and any deep-rooted, more concerning problems that may be underlying these feelings.

If you still have niggling feelings of doubt after you've done all of the research and weighing up, it might be a sign that there are still some underlying issues that need to be addressed. Perhaps you might not be emotionally ready for university yet. Or, deep down, perhaps you're still tempted to take up that internship for school-leavers at X Company. Make sure that you're attuned to these feelings, so that you can acknowledge and address them, one way or the other.

Upon submission, you should feel a sense of satisfaction and relief that you've made the best possible decision you can make without the benefit of hindsight. You can then forget all about university applications and get on with your life. And by getting on with life, I mean working your butt off to achieve the grades for your offers!

6.) CONCLUSION

YOU DID IT!

Congratulations. Having read through the entirety of this book, you should now be in the position where you've chosen the university that you wish to attend, and have sent your UCAS application off accordingly. Rest assured, provided that you have followed the principles outlined in this book, you can relax knowing full well that you have made the best possible decision.

The journey of choosing a university has come to an end. However, your time with me doesn't have to end here. This book has an accompanying website at howtochooseauniversity.com that you're free to check out. It's worth checking the website out even if you have now made a decision about which university to attend, as it will contain a bunch of material that will be useful for when you are at university.

I also invite you to check out my website, *Louis Tee*, where you can find more insights and advice relating to school and university, as well many other different topics such as travelling, relationships and personal development. You can access it at: louistee.com. I'll repeat what I said at the outset in the foreword; thank you *so* much for purchasing this book, and I hope that you have found it useful.

One favour to ask...

Wait up! Just before you leave, I have one favour to ask. If you have found this book useful, please spread the word about it with other people that may benefit from reading it. I'm just a regular 21 year-old, and any additional purchases would mean *so* much to me.

One more favour to ask...

One other thing that you could do for me is to please, please leave a review. It does a great deal of good for my exposure on these gigantic websites such as Amazon and what not.

THANK YOU. NOW GO AND HAVE A BLAST AT UNIVERSITY!

Notes

Printed in Great Britain
by Amazon